CHARTING YOUR
PATH TO
PROFESSIONAL SUCCESS

Title
Charting Your Path to Professional Success

Subtitles
- A Seven-Step Guide for Job Seekers and Entrepreneurs
- Empowering Professionals Through Technology & Personal Branding

Author
Max Haroon

Cover Design
Kashif Iqbal

Publisher
The Healthy Aging Foundation

Book Website
https://healthyaging.foundation/

ISBN-13

Paperback: 9798863065250

Disclaimer

This book is intended as a general educational guide. The views and opinions expressed are based on my personal experience.

While the resources listed are current and relevant at present, they may change in time, beyond our control.

The reader is advised to apply his/her own judgement in all cases.

In Praise of this Book

"I was pleasantly surprised to find that Max has addressed to topic so well from 7 different perspectives. These not only address the needs of the career seeker, but provide a valuable guide to the professional life of anybody at any time. His wisdom goes well beyond what one usually encounters in career works. I would recommend this book to anybody looking for a career change, especially new immigrants."

Duke Duyck
Retired Professional Engineer and Profitability Analyst/Consultant

~~~~~~

"A Seven-Step Guide for Jobseekers and Entrepreneurs is a beacon for those navigating the challenging terrains of professional growth and entrepreneurial success. With its pragmatic approach and a plethora of resources, this book is a must-read for anyone looking to transform their aspirations into reality. Truly a game-changer!"

Kashif Iqbal, MD
Neuro Corporate Strategist, Mental Health Architect

~~~~~~

"Charting Your Professional Success Path: A Seven-Step Guide for Job Seekers and Entrepreneurs" is a wonderful guide to bring us distracted lost people back to our basic self.

The book should be compulsory reading material not only to all immigrants to Canada and other countries, but to all those who face any kind of crisis in their lives. Congratulations on this wake up call."

Mazahir Rahim
Legacy Filmmaker, Founder, Rahim Films

Preface

The starting point of all achievement is desire." - Napoleon Hill

This book is the product of my extensive experience delivering talks at diverse conferences and job fairs. While it wasn't my initial intention, my focus naturally gravitated towards newcomers and recent graduates—individuals who are not only new to their careers but also often new to a country. Perhaps this inclination stems from my personal journey, having transitioned from Engineering to the field of Technology and traversed continents in pursuit of my goals.

While the initial edition of this book was penned between 2007 and 2012. The professional landscape has evolved, driven by technology and the emergence of social media, yet the bedrock principles that underpin professional success have not changed.

In this Revised Edition, I have retained the structure while introducing updated insights and pertinent resources for 2023. The objective remains unchanged: to empower you with strategies that transcend time, empowering your journey in a dynamic professional world.

As you journey through the pages of this book, you'll encounter actionable insights and guidance designed to elevate your career, whether you're a newcomer, a recent graduate, an aspiring entrepreneur, or someone in the midst of a career transition. We're excited to join you on this transformative path, and we trust that the wisdom shared herein will empower you to achieve new heights of professional success.

A plethora of online resources is available to complement the strategies outlined in this book as Appendices of the book. These resources are easily accessible, with many of them being offered free of charge.

I would be immensely grateful if you could offer feedback or contribute to future editions. As a gesture of appreciation, I am happy to send you a copy of one of my books. Currently, most of my writings delve into the realms of holistic medicine and integrative health.

For more of my articles and writings, please visit my Webfolio by following the link to my publications at: http://www.maxharoon.org/

Wishing you success on your journey!

Dedication

This book is dedicated to all the young and shy individuals, inspiring them to break free from their shells and proudly reveal their potential.

"Everything you've ever wanted is on the other side of fear."
- George Addair

The Book Workshops

Two engaging workshops, inspired by the book, are now open for community organizations and educational institutions:

1. The first workshop delves into effective pitching, navigating in-person scenarios, and leveraging the online resources featured in the book.

2. The second workshop is exclusively designed for entrepreneurs, offering insights into a wide array of tools to harness the power of technology.

To check if your organization is eligible for these workshops, please reach out to the author or the Healthy Aging Foundation.

Table of Contents

Chapters

Appendices

Chapter 1

Introduction

"Success is not the key to happiness. Happiness is the key to success. If you love what you are doing, you will be successful."

- Albert Schweitzer

"This book serves as your ultimate guide to success, providing a straightforward seven-step strategy that is adaptable to a wide range of scenarios. Whether you're on the hunt for a job, advancing in your career, managing a business, or embarking on an entrepreneurial journey, the tips and techniques outlined here are versatile and highly effective. They're equally applicable whether you're in familiar territory or exploring new horizons.

Achieving success requires a well-rounded approach. It means not only assessing your personal traits, your strengths and weeknesses, but also evaluating your strategies. If your current approach isn't yielding the desired results, it's time to broaden your perspective. Success often involves stepping back and looking at the bigger picture.

Let's break it down further: Imagine you're in search of a job, and despite possessing an impressive resume and qualifications, you're struggling to secure the right position. That's when it becomes essential to consider the broader context. Employers seek candidates who not only meet job requirements but also seamlessly integrate into their company's culture.

If you're new to Canada or undergoing a career change, you may be wondering how to succeed and fit in seamlessly. Drawing from my extensive career journey spanning the UK to Canada, which includes delivering talks and presentations at various job fairs and community organizations, I've developed a comprehensive seven-step strategy for career success. This strategy can be applied to every aspect of your professional journey.

Having experienced both sides of the employment equation, as both a jobseeker and an employer, I've crafted a comprehensive seven-step strategy for professional success. These seven steps are as follows:

Step 1: Self-Promotion & Establishing Credibility
Step 2: Networking (Social and Business)
Step 3: Attitude & Acculturation
Step 4: Volunteering
Step 5: Mentoring & Coaching
Step 6: Lifelong Learning
Step 7: Harmonizing Life and Living

Chapter 2

Self-Promotion &
Establishing Credibility

"The future depends on what you do today."
- Mahatma Gandhi

In a vibrant city, two software developers, Lisa and John, were pursuing their careers in the competitive tech industry.

Lisa was a brilliant coder with a passion for creating innovative software solutions. She spent most of her time behind her computer screen, working on complex projects. Lisa believed that her work should speak for itself and that self-promotion was unnecessary. She rarely shared her achievements, seldom attended industry events, and didn't engage with the tech community online.

John, on the other hand, recognized the significance of self-promotion and credibility. He actively participated in coding forums; sharing his knowledge and helping others troubleshoot coding challenges. He attended tech meetups, hackathons, and conferences, where he networked with fellow developers, entrepreneurs, and industry leaders. John also maintained a blog and contributed articles to tech publications, showcasing his expertise.

Over time, John's online presence grew, and he became known as a reliable source of information and a problem solver in the coding community. Employers and recruiters took notice of his contributions, and he received offers for exciting job opportunities.

Lisa, despite her exceptional coding skills, faced difficulties in advancing her career. She realized that her reluctance to self-promote and establish credibility was holding her back. Determined to change her approach, she started a tech blog, shared her coding achievements on social media, and began attending tech conferences.

As Lisa actively engaged with the tech community, her reputation began to flourish. She started receiving recognition for her work, and job offers and freelance opportunities started pouring in.

Introduction

The story of Lisa and John underscores the importance of self-promotion and establishing credibility in the competitive professional landscape. While skills are essential, actively sharing your expertise, networking, and building a positive reputation can significantly enhance your career prospects and open doors to new opportunities.

Think about what business professionals do to sell their products or services. They advertise, promote themselves vigorously, and actively seek publicity. If these methods have stood the test of time, why aren't you, as a professional, leveraging them? You might argue that you have nothing to sell, but I'd counter that by saying, "You have to sell yourself."

In your career journey, you wear the dual hats of both the business and the product. This realization underscores the importance of possessing unwavering self-confidence and self-esteem. You must promote yourself as the finest product in the market. To do this effectively, you need to establish and communicate the business value you bring to the table. Show employers, customers, and colleagues how they will benefit from your unique blend of services and skills.

The beauty of the digital age lies in the accessibility of the Internet, often the most cost-effective means to achieve self-promotion and gain publicity. Embrace the power of the Internet to bolster your professional image. Here are some initial ideas to set you on the right path. When a prospective employer, customer, or colleague decides to "Google you," make sure they encounter a comprehensive and impressive portrayal of your professional self.

This chapter explores three distinct tools and platforms for self-promotion and the establishment of your professional credibility:

(a) Creating Your Personal Domain
(b) Participating in Online Forums/Groups
(c) Establishing Credibility

We will conclude this chapter by providing you with resources for self-promotion and credibility. Additional resources are provided in the Appendices.

Creating Your Personal Domain

It's a digital reflection of your identity in the professional world. One key step to consider is registering your own domain name, which not only gives you a unique web address but also opens the door to using a personalized email address associated with that domain.

My domain and its website is http://maxharoon.org/

My email address is contact@maxharoon.org , which presents a more professional image on my business card than contact@hotmail.com. Many job seekers use email addresses provided by their Internet Service Providers (e.g., Bell, BT, and Verizon) or email services (e.g., Google, Hotmail). However, by having your email linked to your own domain, you gain several advantages.

Firstly, you no longer need to fret about canceling your ISP service. Your email address remains yours as long as you continue to renew your domain name and hosting service. This means you have a permanent, professional email address that isn't dependent on your ISP's availability.

Setting up your domain name is a straightforward process that typically involves a small annual fee. Do a Google search "How to register a domain"; some resources for free domain registration are provided in the Appendices.

By owning your domain and email address, you're sending a clear signal to the professional world that you're serious about your career and ready to stand out.

If you perform a search using Google, Bing, or Yahoo for the best and free web hosting companies, you will find a lengthy list. Your task will be to compare them and choose the most suitable one.

Blogging offers not one, but two avenues for promoting yourself professionally. The first approach involves providing insightful feedback and comments on other people's blogs. The second, and equally effective method, is to create your very own blog. The best part? Creating your blog is easy, and it won't cost you a dime.

When you register to create a blog, you'll be assigned a unique URL, akin to having your own website without the need to register a domain name or host it yourself. For instance, your URL could look something like maxharoon.blogspot.com. The process of creating your blog is hassle-free and, most importantly, free of charge.

To embark on your blogging journey, head over to blogspot.com. There, you can set up your blog with ease and start sharing your thoughts and expertise with the world. Whether you choose to comment on existing blogs or establish your platform, blogging is a potent tool for self-promotion, networking, and showcasing your professional acumen.

There are many other free blogging services and resources to create them that you can search for on the internet.

Participating in Online Forums/Groups

Online forums are invaluable hubs where you can delve into a wide array of topics, from technical and economic matters to social and political issues. Within these digital spaces, you have the opportunity to engage in lively discussions, share your interests, and become part of online communities. Much like the world of blogging, participating in online forums allows you to amplify your professional presence.

To get started, consider joining existing online forums or groups that align with your interests and expertise. You can start with social media websites as most of them thrive on postings and others commenting on them. There are a large number of forums, message boards, and online communities available on the internet.

You can find a list of these resources in Appendix F.

By participating actively in these online forums and groups, you not only gain valuable insights but also establish your presence in your chosen field. Networking and building connections become natural outcomes of your engagement, further enhancing your professional profile.

Establishing Credibility

In the world of professional and business success, your reputation is paramount. It is intrinsically linked to your visibility in the job market or the business arena. Enhanced credibility not only magnifies your presence but also brings your skills, talents, and business services into sharper focus.

Here are several strategies to help you solidify your credibility in your chosen field of expertise:

1. Publishing Articles, E-Books, and Books

Sharing your knowledge through the written word is a powerful method to position yourself as an authority. Whether it's crafting articles, e-books, or full-length books, publishing allows you to showcase your expertise while imparting valuable insights to your audience.

2. Speaking at Events and Professional Gatherings

Public speaking engagements provide a platform to not only disseminate your knowledge but also to connect with peers and potential clients. Participation in conferences, seminars, and professional meetings positions you as a thought leader and an indispensable contributor to your field.

3. Leveraging Internet Resources

Harness the vast reach of the internet to augment your credibility. Consider publishing e-zines, e-newsletters, or writing white papers that highlight your expertise and offer valuable solutions to your target audience.

By adopting these strategies, you can strengthen your credibility, ensuring that your skills and talents shine brightly in your professional or business journey.

Resources for Self-Promotion and Credibility

1. LinkedIn

Create a strong LinkedIn profile showcasing your professional background, skills, and accomplishments. Engage in industry-related discussions, share valuable content, and connect with peers and potential employers.

2. Personal Website or Blog

Develop a personal website or blog where you can regularly publish articles, insights, and industry-related content. Sharing your knowledge and expertise through a blog can help establish you as an authority in your field.

3. Online Courses and Certifications

Enroll in online courses and certifications relevant to your profession. Platforms like Coursera, edX, and LinkedIn Learning offer a wide range of courses that can enhance your skills and credibility.

4. Social Media

Utilize social media platforms such as Twitter, Facebook, and Instagram to share professional insights, network with industry leaders, and participate in relevant discussions.

5. Professional Associations

Join industry-specific professional associations and organizations. Many of these associations have online communities and forums where you can connect with peers and contribute to discussions.

6. Research and Publications

Contribute to online research publications, journals, or industry-specific websites. Sharing your research and insights can establish you as an expert in your field.

7. Online Webinars and Podcasts

Host webinars or participate in podcast interviews to share your expertise and knowledge with a broader audience.

8. Online Portfolio

Create an online portfolio showcasing your work, projects, and achievements. Platforms like Behance, GitHub, or a personal website can serve as a digital showcase of your skills.

9. Online Forums and Q&A Sites

 Participate in industry-related forums such as Quora or Stack Exchange to answer questions, provide valuable advice, and connect with professionals in your field.

10. Guest Blogging

Write guest posts for reputable industry blogs and websites. Guest blogging allows you to reach a wider audience and gain credibility within your niche.

11. Online Reviews and Recommendations

Encourage clients or colleagues to leave positive reviews and recommendations on platforms like LinkedIn or industry-specific review sites.

Remember that consistency and quality are keys when utilizing these online resources to establish your professional credibility. Regularly update your profiles, engage with your audience, and share valuable insights to build trust and recognition within your industry.

Chapter 3

Social and Business Networking

"Your time is limited; don't waste it living someone else's life."
- Steve Jobs

I'd like to kick off this chapter by sharing two personal stories, each highlighting the significance of networking, both socially and in the business context.

The first tale takes us back about five decades when I resided in London, England. During the Christmas season, I found myself on my own and, when asked about my plans, I confessed it would be just another ordinary day. To my surprise, a kind soul at a Rotary Club Christmas event extended an invitation to spend Christmas with his family. I gladly accepted, and that festive day turned into a cherished memory, complete with new family contacts.

Fast forward two decades to Toronto, Canada. As a founder of an Internet Association, I was attending a conference, naturally gravitating towards the exposition area and engaging in networking with fellow attendees. Among them were a couple of individuals from the USA, and after exchanging business cards, one of them inquired if I could assist in establishing their company's branch in Canada. We agreed to meet the following day at their hotel. During our discussion, I not only pledged my support but also outlined the potential demand for their services in Canada. To cut a long story short, the endeavour blossomed into a highly successful company that exceeded its projected revenue within the first year.

These anecdotes underscore the immense value of networking, whether in pursuit of job opportunities or the establishment of prosperous businesses.

Introduction

In the fiercely competitive landscape of the 21st century, the importance of cultivating your own network cannot be overstated. Whether you're seeking business opportunities, job openings, or the right employees, networking is often the key to unlocking these hidden avenues. Remarkably, it's estimated that a staggering 80% of jobs or contracts are never advertised, residing in what's aptly termed the "hidden job market." Paradoxically, more than 80% of job seekers focus their efforts solely on applying for "advertised" jobs, leading to intense competition for these positions.

The business world has long recognized the power of "Word of Mouth" as the most effective marketing method. So, why not apply this concept to individuals? To do so, immerse yourself in a multitude of events. Let everyone in your network know that you're actively "seeking" opportunities, whether they pertain to jobs, business ventures, or recruitment needs. Clearly communicate your key skills and the business services you provide.

Consider becoming a member of networking organizations tailored to your industry or interests. These platforms offer invaluable opportunities to forge connections, exchange ideas, and identify potential collaborators or clients.

This chapter explores three distinct tools and platforms for self-promotion and the establishment of your professional credibility:

(a) Join a Local Networking Group
(b) Plan to Attend Events
(c) What to do After the Event

We will conclude this chapter by providing you with resources to find events. Additional resources are provided in the Appendices.

Join a Local Networking Group

There are many organizations like Speakers Clubs, Local Business Associations, and Business Networking International (BNI) where you can learn the art of speaking and networking. While you may not find some in your area, there is a good likelihood of finding a local Toastmasters Club. With approximately 20,000 clubs worldwide, you're likely to find one right in your city or neighborhood.

For a nominal annual fee, joining this organization offers a plethora of benefits:

- **Networking Opportunities**

  Toastmasters provides an excellent platform for networking with local individuals while enhancing your English language proficiency and networking skills.

- **Enhanced Communication**

You'll learn the art of giving compelling speeches, a skill that's invaluable when someone asks you to "Tell me something about yourself." This ability to craft and deliver engaging personal pitches can be a game-changer.

- **Improved Public Speaking**

  Toastmasters is renowned for helping individuals improve their public speaking skills. Whether you're addressing a small group or a large audience, you'll gain confidence and proficiency.

- **Leadership Development**

  In addition to public speaking, Toastmasters offers opportunities to build leadership skills. You can take on roles within the club, such as serving as an officer or organizing events, to hone your leadership abilities.

- **Unlock Your Potential**

  Toastmasters is a place where you can maximize your potential. You'll receive constructive feedback from your peers, helping you identify areas for improvement and continuously grow.

Joining a local Toastmasters Club isn't just about professional development; it's about personal growth and empowerment. It's a supportive environment where you can refine your communication and leadership abilities while connecting with like-minded individuals.

Don't miss out on this incredible opportunity to invest in yourself and your future. Locate a Toastmasters Club near you and embark on a journey of self-improvement and self-expression. You'll appreciate the significance of these resources, especially considering that nearly all universities and colleges in the USA and Canada have either a Toastmaster Club or a TEDx Club.

To discover the nearest Toastmasters Group, visit http://www.toastmasters.org

Plan to Attend Events

Regularly attending events is a fantastic way to build and nurture your network. Conferences, seminars, tradeshows, association meetings, and community gatherings take place daily, particularly in and around Toronto. However, before you become a social butterfly, it's crucial to approach events strategically. Research the event to gauge its relevance to your objectives, and then prepare a plan to maximize your participation.

Here are some practical recommendations to excel in networking at events:

- **Initiating Conversations**

  Walking into a room filled with strangers can be daunting for many. However, it's essential to remember that many attendees likely share your discomfort. Start by making eye contact with someone in the room, offer a warm smile, and approach them with a handshake. As you introduce yourself, maintain a comfortable distance. This gesture is often sufficient to break the ice. If not, initiate a conversation with a non-threatening question related to the event, such as, "What are your thoughts on the speaker?" or "Are you a part of this organization?" Confidence is key, so don't be a passive spectator; take charge of the situation by being proactive.

- **Craft a 30-Second Elevator Pitch**

  When someone inquires about your profession be prepared to articulate your strengths and capabilities succinctly in a 30-second elevator pitch. Practice this pitch daily, as it serves as the verbal equivalent of your business card and resume. You can also have a basic pitch that you customize based on the context. Keep it concise, as the purpose of an elevator pitch is to pique the listener's interest and encourage them to learn more about you.

- **Carry Business Cards**

  Even if you are not currently employed, having business cards is crucial, especially during this phase of your life. Consider printing a brief profile or five bulleted lines at the back of your card. The front of the card can display your website and blog addresses.

- **Adopt a Networking Attitude - Givers Gain**

  Building a reputation as a contributor and helper in your network is highly valuable. Show genuine interest in others and be open to providing assistance when you can. Remember, what you give often comes back to you in unexpected ways.

- **Avoid Prejudgment**

  Never prejudge anyone you encounter at events. Each person you meet knows approximately 250 people, and among them might be someone who can significantly impact your career or business goals. Treat everyone with respect and openness.

- **Be Interesting and Interested**

  Cultivate the ability to be engaging and genuinely interested in others. People are drawn to those who show curiosity and enthusiasm in conversations.

- **Network Widely and Enjoyably**

  Embrace networking as a joyful pursuit. Network with enthusiasm and connect with people from all walks of life, everywhere you go. Networking should be an enjoyable experience, so have fun while doing it.

What to do after an Event

Your networking efforts don't end when the event concludes; in fact, what you do afterward is just as crucial. Here's a post-event action plan to maximize the value of your networking interactions:

1. Create a Contact Database

Organize the contacts you've made at the event by creating a computerized database. You can use basic address book tools like Outlook, contact management systems such as ACT, or customer relationship management (CRM) platforms like freecrm.com. Categorize contacts by industry, profession, or any other relevant criteria to streamline your follow-ups.

2. Send a "Nice to Meet You" Message

When someone sends you a referral or recommends you, remember to thank them right away. A quick thank you note via email or text is all that is needed. And let them know if it leads to something good happening!

3. Regular Follow-Ups

Keep the momentum going by staying in touch with your prospects every 30-45 days. Share relevant content, updates, or simply check in to see how they're doing. Consistent and meaningful follow-ups maintain and strengthen your connections.

4. Acknowledge Referrals

When someone in your network sends you a referral or recommendation, promptly acknowledge their contribution. Express your gratitude in writing, be it through email, a thank-you letter, or a phone call. Keep them informed about the progress or outcome resulting from their referral.

5. Persistence Pays Off

Remember that effective networking involves consistent follow-up. Don't underestimate the power of follow-up; it's where relationships deepen and opportunities emerge. Be persistent, but also respectful of your contacts' time and preferences.

In the world of networking, the post-event phase is where you turn initial connections into enduring relationships. By maintaining communication, showing appreciation, and delivering value, you'll maximize the potential of your networking efforts.

Resources to Find Events

There are indeed countless places and opportunities for networking. Networking isn't confined to formal events; it can happen anywhere you interact with people. Here are a few online resources.

1. Meetup (meetup.com)

Meetup is a platform that helps people find and build local communities. You can search for groups or events related to your interests, hobbies, or professional goals, and then attend in-person gatherings.

2. Eventbrite (eventbrite.com)

Eventbrite is a popular platform for discovering and creating events. You can search for local events, conferences, workshops, and networking meetups based on your preferences and location.

3. LinkedIn Events

LinkedIn offers an "Events" feature where you can discover and RSVP to professional events, seminars, workshops, and conferences in your area. It's a great way to connect with other professionals attending the same events.

4. Facebook Groups

Many local Facebook Groups focus on specific interests, industries, or communities. Joining relevant groups can help you stay informed about local events and networking opportunities.

5. Eventful (eventful.com)

Eventful is an event discovery platform that allows you to search for events by location and category. You can find a wide range of local gatherings, including business networking events. Eventful is an event discovery platform that lets you search for events based on location and interests. It's a great way to find local gatherings and networking events.

6. Professional Association Websites

If you're part of a professional association or organization, check their website for information on local chapter events and meetings. Many associations host regular networking events.

7. Local Chamber of Commerce

Your local Chamber of Commerce often organizes networking events, business mixers, and workshops. Check their website or contact them directly to inquire about upcoming events.

Remember that while online resources are valuable for discovering in-person networking events, the real networking happens when you attend these gatherings and engage with fellow attendees face-to-face.

Chapter 4

Attitude & Acculturation

"The best way to predict the future is to create it." - Peter Drucker

This story brings to mind an incident from a few years ago when I used to give talks at job fairs in Toronto. Following one of my presentations, an attendee approached me with a question, "Mr. Haroon, I'm a newly arrived immigrant from India, and despite my qualifications and education – I even hold a Ph.D. in my field – I'm struggling to find a job here. Why is that?"

After a brief conversation, I asked him, "Do you genuinely want to know the answer?" He replied, "Yes."

I explained that employers often have to sift through a high volume of applications, and as a result, they tend to focus more on rejecting candidates than hiring them. I referred to these factors as "Rejection Factors." I then asked him if he knew what his rejection factors were, and he admitted that he didn't.

I told him that one of his rejection factors was his English proficiency. I suggested that he consider taking English conversation and accent reduction classes. Initially, he was a bit defensive and questioned, "Is my English really that bad?" I assured him that his English was quite good, but we were discussing the nuances of colloquial and spoken Canadian English.

This story underscores the importance of acculturation and having the willingness to adapt, highlighting the significance of attitude in accepting necessary changes for professional success.

This chapter explores two aspects of acculturation:

(a) Rejection Factors
(b) Adaptation and Conformity

Additional resources are provided in the Appendices.

Rejection Factors

To embark on this transformative journey, it's crucial to appreciate the nuanced perspective of those who make hiring decisions. Hiring managers face a daunting challenge - an overwhelming influx of applications, often beyond their capacity to thoroughly evaluate. Paradoxically, this surplus of applications turns the process into one primarily focused on eliminating candidate efficiently.

This may seem counterintuitive, but it's a pivotal insight for job seekers to grasp. The goal, then, is to minimize "rejection factors" that can inadvertently hinder your progress.

What do these Rejection Factors (RF) entail? They encompass a wide array of elements, including physical traits and characteristics that can unintentionally influence hiring choices:

- **Grooming**

  Your overall presentation and how you carry yourself.

- **Physical Appearance**

  Unfortunately, this includes factors related to minority status and gender, which can influence perceptions.

- **Communication Skills**

  How you articulate your thoughts and ideas, both in pronunciation and expression.

- **Attire**

  Your choice of clothing and how it aligns with the culture of the organization.

This book aims to bolster your prospects of success by offering strategies to minimize or mitigate your RF, ensuring you're recognized for your skills, qualifications, and potential rather than being unintentionally sidelined by factors outside your control.

Adaptation and Conformity

Now, let's expand on the networking attitude to include your overall attitude. A positive attitude, both towards yourself and life in general, is vital for success in interviews, business meetings, and your career as a whole. Maintaining a positive outlook is essential, and here are some strategies to help you cultivate and sustain it:

- **Read Inspirational Books**

  Explore the world of inspirational literature. Books that offer wisdom, motivation, and insight can have a profound impact on your attitude and mindset. Seek out reading materials that resonate with you and uplift your spirits.

- **Meditation and Quiet Reflection**

  Dedicate a few minutes each day to meditation or quiet reflection. Find a sanctuary or a favorite place where you can retreat for peaceful contemplation. These moments of stillness can help you center yourself and maintain a positive mindset.

- **Surround Yourself with Encouragement**

  Keep company with close friends and companions who support, encourage, and motivate you. Positive relationships and a strong support system can be invaluable in maintaining a positive attitude.

For those in environments or countries that are not native to them, acculturation becomes a crucial aspect of adapting and thriving. Just as each country has its unique culture and language, every industry has its own jargon and culture. Understanding and adapting to the culture of both your workplace and your industry is essential. Recognize that a country's culture has multiple layers, including geographical, political, work-related, and social dimensions.

If you receive a rejection regarding a job offer, it's essential to perform a self-examination. Consider whether you may have conveyed, intentionally or inadvertently, that you lack certain qualities or attributes that organizations value. These qualities might include:

- **Industry Awareness**

  Demonstrating a strong grasp of industry trends and staying informed about developments in your field is crucial.

- **Teamwork**

  Emphasize your ability to collaborate and contribute effectively within a team environment.

- **Communication Skills**

  Articulate communication, both verbal and written, is highly regarded by employers.

- **High Potential**

  Present yourself as someone with a high potential for growth and development within the organization.

- **Cultural Adaptability**

  In an increasingly diverse world, showcasing cultural sensitivity and adaptability can set you apart.

Remember that culture has many layers, encompassing geographical, political, work-related, and social elements. Your ability to navigate and adapt to these various cultural dimensions can significantly influence your success and acceptance in a new environment.

Chapter 5

Volunteering

"Success usually comes to those who are too busy to be looking for it."
- Henry David Thoreau

Volunteering is akin to stepping through the door of opportunity. Have you ever pondered why highly educated university students are willing to go the extra mile to support a political party or association? It's because it adds a feather to your resume's cap, alongside all the valuable contacts you establish during your volunteer service.

During my time managing an association, I had the privilege of working with many dedicated volunteers. When some of them approached me for references to present to prospective employers, I was more than happy to oblige.

I dare say that nurturing the habit of volunteering should be a lifelong pursuit. If you haven't already started, now is an excellent time to begin.

Introduction

One effective way to broaden your horizons and expand your network is through volunteering. It's an invaluable avenue for gaining experience and demonstrating your commitment, particularly if you've ever been told, "You lack Canadian or relevant experience." Volunteering or seeking internships can help bridge that gap.

Volunteering not only benefits others but also enhances your character and professional development. By giving your time and skills to causes you're passionate about, you demonstrate your dedication to potential employers and influential individuals in your field.

Volunteering is essential for your career for several reasons:

1. Skill Development

Volunteering allows you to acquire and enhance various skills, which can be valuable in your professional life. You can learn teamwork, leadership, communication, problem-solving, and project management skills through volunteer activities.

2. Networking Opportunities

Volunteering often puts you in contact with people from various backgrounds and industries. Building a strong network can open doors to job opportunities, mentorship, and collaborations.

3. Resume Enhancement

Including volunteer experience on your resume demonstrates your commitment to personal growth and community involvement. Employers often value candidates who contribute to their communities.

4. Demonstrating Values

Volunteering showcases your values and interests outside of work. Employers may look favorably on candidates who are socially responsible and dedicated to making a positive impact.

5. Gaining Experience

For individuals new to a field, volunteering can provide hands-on experience and help bridge the gap between education and employment.

6. Confidence Building

Volunteering can boost your confidence and self-esteem, making you more self-assured in job interviews and professional interactions.

7. Exploring Career Paths

Volunteering in different roles or organizations can help you explore various career paths and industries before committing to a specific job or career change.

8. References and Recommendations

Volunteering can lead to valuable references and recommendations from supervisors or colleagues who can vouch for your skills and dedication.

9. Filling Employment Gaps

If you have gaps in your employment history, volunteering can help fill those gaps, showing that you remained engaged and active during periods of unemployment.

10. Personal Fulfillment

Volunteering can be personally fulfilling and provide a sense of purpose. Happy and content individuals often perform better in their careers.

In summary, volunteering offers a myriad of benefits that can significantly impact your professional growth and career success. Whether you're looking to develop new skills, expand your network, or give back to your community, volunteering can be a valuable asset in your career journey.

Where to Volunteer

You can volunteer in a variety of organizations and causes depending on your interests and goals. Here are some common places to volunteer and the reasons why you might consider them:

1. Local Non-profits

Volunteering for local non-profit organizations can help your community directly. You can assist with food banks, shelters, or organizations that support children, seniors, or people with disabilities. Volunteering locally allows you to see the immediate impact of your efforts.

2. Hospitals and Healthcare Facilities

Volunteering in healthcare settings can provide valuable experience if you're pursuing a career in medicine or healthcare. You can assist with patient care, administrative tasks, or support services.

3. Schools and Educational Programs

Volunteering in schools or educational programs can benefit students and educators. You can tutor, mentor, or help with extracurricular activities. It's an excellent choice if you're passionate about education.

4. Environmental Organizations

If you care about the environment, consider volunteering with conservation groups, wildlife reserves, or community clean-up initiatives. Your efforts can contribute to a cleaner and greener world.

5. Animal Shelters

Animal lovers often find fulfillment in volunteering at animal shelters or rescue organizations. You can help care for animals, assist with adoptions, or raise awareness about animal welfare.

6. Professional Associations

Joining professional associations related to your field or industry can provide opportunities for networking, skill development, and advancing your career. Many associations have volunteer roles, such as organizing events or mentoring newcomers.

7. Disaster Relief Organizations

Disaster relief organizations like the Red Cross provide critical assistance during emergencies. Volunteering in disaster response can be emotionally rewarding and a way to help communities in crisis.

8. Community Events and Festivals

Many communities host events and festivals that rely on volunteers for planning, organization, and execution. These events can be fun to participate in and offer a chance to connect with your community.

9. Global Volunteer Programs

Some people choose to volunteer abroad with international organizations. This option allows you to experience different cultures, make a global impact, and gain a broader perspective on global issues.

10. Online Volunteering

Virtual volunteering opportunities are available for those with limited time or mobility. You can assist with online research, content creation, or support non-profit organizations remotely.

11. Companies in Your Industry

Some companies offer internship programs for individuals looking to gain hands-on experience in their industry. Research and reach out to organizations in your field to explore internship opportunities.

Reasons to volunteer can vary widely, but some common motivations include giving back to the community, learning new skills, building your resume, expanding your network, making a positive impact, and finding personal fulfillment. When choosing where to volunteer, consider your interests, skills, and the causes that resonate with you the most.

So, seize the opportunity to make a positive impact and grow both personally and professionally through volunteering

Chapter 6

Mentoring & Coaching

"The only thing that stands between you and your dream is the will to try and the belief that it is actually possible."
- Joel Brown

Take the story of Vincent Lam, an emergency room doctor in Toronto. His journey as an author might have never begun if he hadn't crossed paths with Margaret Atwood, a renowned Canadian author. The opportunity happened while they were on a cruise ship. Margaret Atwood became Vincent's mentor, offering guidance and support for his manuscript and helping bring his book to publication. According to Vincent Lam, his book, titled "Bloodletting and Other Miraculous Cures," would not have seen the light of day without Margaret Atwood's unwavering mentorship.

Under Margaret Atwood's tutelage, not only did his book get published, but it also went on to earn several prestigious literary accolades. This story serves as a testament to the transformative power of mentorship.

Having a mentor can be a game-changer in your journey towards success. They provide valuable insights, share their wisdom, and offer critical guidance. They are a source of motivation, accountability, and inspiration, pushing you to reach heights you might never have thought possible.

Introduction

On our journey toward success, we all require guidance and wisdom from individuals who can inspire and steer us toward our goals. However, we often overlook the importance of seeking out mentors and coaches in both our personal and professional lives.

In my presentation, "A Seven-Step Strategy for Professional Success," I emphasize the significance of having three essential figures in your life: **A Mentor**

    a)   **A Business Coach/Career Coach:**
    b)   **A Technical Coach**

We will conclude by considering other aspects of Mentoring:

- Your own Team of Advisors
- You as a Mentor
- How to Find a Mentor or Coach

A Mentor

A mentor is like a guiding light, an experienced individual who can offer insights, share their knowledge, and provide valuable advice. Mentors inspire, challenge, and help you navigate the complexities of your career and life.

It's often said that behind every successful person lies a secret idol or mentor. Some even go as far as hanging their mentor's picture as a constant reminder of the mentor's achievements and a wellspring of inspiration and motivation.

So, consider seeking out your own mentor, someone whose experiences and achievements resonate with you. Having a mentor can make all the difference in your pursuit of professional and personal excellence.

In the good old days, close-knit families and shared living with elders were the norm. Your mentors were your grandparents and uncles. Unfortunately, we no longer have those wise resources readily available.

10 Best TED talks on Mentorship:
https://www.growthmentor.com/blog/ted-talks-on-mentorship/

A Business or Career Coach

A business or career coach is not merely an advisor; they are your strategic partner in the journey of professional development. Their role goes far beyond offering casual advice; they are instrumental in helping you set and achieve concrete goals, refine your skill set, and surmount the obstacles that may lay in your path. A coach provides structured, personalized guidance to elevate your career trajectory.

Consider this: When you aim to improve your performance in hockey, tennis, or golf, you don't think twice about hiring a coach. You recognize that their expertise can fine-tune your game, help you identify areas of improvement, and guide you toward excellence. In the same vein, why not harness the power of a Business Coach or Career Coach to elevate your professional life?

Here's why you should seriously consider it:

1. **Enhanced Performance**

Just as a sports coach can refine your technique and tactics, a business or career coach can enhance your performance in the workplace. They help you identify and capitalize on your strengths, while also addressing areas that may need development.

2. **Risk Mitigation**

Coaches have a unique ability to spot potential risks or pitfalls in your career or business endeavors. They offer insights and strategies to minimize these risks, ultimately safeguarding your long-term success.

3. **Skill Development**

Your coach will work with you to develop critical business and career skills that you may not currently possess or even realize you need. They can help you bridge skill gaps and stay ahead in a constantly evolving professional landscape.

4. **Cost-Effective Investment**

While you might hesitate at the prospect of hiring a coach due to the associated cost, the truth is that their services are an investment that can save you money many times over. They help you make informed decisions, avoid costly mistakes, and optimize your resources effectively.

In essence, a Business Coach or Career Coach is a partner in your pursuit of excellence. They provide guidance, challenge your thinking, and hold you accountable to your goals. With their support, you can reach new heights in your professional journey and achieve the success you aspire to.

The value they bring to your career or business is immeasurable, making them a worthwhile investment that can yield significant returns.

A Digital/Technology Coach

In today's fast-paced world, keeping pace with evolving digital platforms and technical skills is crucial. A digital technology coach is a specialized expert in your field who can help you hone your technical abilities, stay updated with industry trends, and excel in your specific domain.

Many entrepreneurs venture into business due to their technical expertise. However, in the course of your entrepreneurial journey, you may encounter projects that require technical knowledge beyond your current expertise. While the ideal solution may be to subcontract these projects to experts, there's a more cost-effective and efficient approach if you're willing to embrace it. All you need is a dose of technical guidance, and these invaluable guides are what I like to call "technical coaches."

Technical coaches won't complete your projects for you, but they are more than willing to impart their knowledge so you can expand your skillset and knowledge base. They play a role similar to that of teachers, providing you with the guidance and insights necessary to tackle technical challenges effectively. However, it's crucial to understand that you'll be the one doing the work and applying the knowledge gained.

Here's why having a technical coach is a valuable asset:

1. **Cost-Efficiency**

    Technical coaches offer a cost-effective alternative to outsourcing projects. Their guidance allows you to develop the skills needed to handle technical aspects independently, saving you resources in the long run.

2. **Knowledge Transfer**

    These coaches are experts in their respective fields and can transfer their specialized knowledge directly to you. This knowledge transfer empowers you to take on diverse technical challenges with confidence.

3. **Personal Growth**

    Learning under the guidance of a technical coach not only boosts your technical proficiency but also fosters personal growth and problem-solving skills. You'll become a more versatile and adaptable professional.

4. **Resource Optimization**
    By investing in your own technical development, you optimize your resources and reduce your dependence on external experts. This self-reliance can lead to more agile and efficient business operations.

In essence, a technical coach is your go-to resource for expanding your technical prowess. They empower you to tackle complex challenges, broaden your skillset, and stay ahead in a rapidly evolving technical landscape. Embracing the guidance of a technical coach can prove invaluable on your journey to entrepreneurial success.

Dr. Atul Gawande has studied this question with a surgeon's precision. He shares what he's found to be the key: having a good coach to provide a more accurate picture of our reality, to instill positive habits of thinking, and to break our actions down and then help us build them back up again. "It's not how good you are now; it's how good you're going to be that really matters," Gawande says:

https://www.ted.com/talks/atul_gawande_want_to_get_great_at_something_get_a_coach

Mentoring is not Coaching

Mentoring and coaching are related concepts but have distinct differences; some of the nuances are given below:

1. Fees

Mentors: Typically, mentors are volunteers driven by a passion to share their knowledge and wisdom. They may be industry experts or seasoned entrepreneurs.

Coaches: Coaches are paid professionals who specialize in their respective fields. However, volunteer parents, as coaches, are also widely recognized for their contributions to children's sports teams. Their coaching training equips them to be highly effective in guiding others.

2. Purpose

Mentoring: Mentoring is typically a long-term relationship where an experienced individual (the mentor) imparts their knowledge, experience, and wisdom to guide the personal and professional development of a less-experienced individual (the mentee). The primary purpose is to help the mentee grow, develop, and achieve their career and life goals.

Coaching: Coaching is usually a shorter-term, task-focused relationship where a coach helps an individual (the coachee) improve specific skills, overcome challenges, and achieve specific goals. The primary purpose is skill enhancement and performance improvement.

3. Scope

Mentoring: Mentoring often covers a broader range of topics, including career advice, personal development, and life skills. It involves sharing personal experiences and offering guidance based on the mentor's own journey.

Coaching: Coaching tends to be more narrowly focused on specific issues or goals, such as improving leadership skills, enhancing time management, or achieving a particular project outcome. It relies on asking questions and guiding the coachee to find their solutions.

4. Feedback

Mentoring: In mentoring, feedback may be less structured and may involve sharing personal anecdotes and experiences to provide guidance.

Coaching: Coaching relies heavily on feedback mechanisms and may involve assessments, evaluations, and performance metrics to measure progress.

5. Duration

Mentoring: Mentorship relationships can be long-term and may continue for an extended period, sometimes even years.

Coaching: Coaching relationships are often shorter and are designed to achieve specific outcomes within a defined timeframe.

In summary, mentoring is more about sharing wisdom and guiding personal development, while coaching is focused on skill improvement and goal achievement. Both are valuable approaches for personal and professional growth, and individuals may benefit from a combination of both, depending on their needs and objectives.

A Word about Heroes

Heroes and mentors serve different roles in our lives. Heroes are often admired for their extraordinary actions or qualities, while mentors provide guidance, support, and wisdom to help us grow and develop in specific areas. While heroes can inspire us, mentors play a more active and direct role in our personal and professional development.

Your Own Team of Advisors

Additionally, if you're an entrepreneur or embarking on a new business venture, consider forming your own Collaboration Team of Mentors or Advisors

This team should ideally comprise professionals from diverse fields, including law, accounting, and fellow entrepreneurs. Initially, seek individuals who are willing to offer their advice and expertise on a pro bono basis. This arrangement allows you to assess the chemistry and compatibility of their working relationship with you.

Building a Business Team of Mentors can be a strategic move in your entrepreneurial journey. These advisors bring a wealth of knowledge and experience to the table, offering invaluable insights and guidance to help you navigate the complexities of entrepreneurship.

By assembling such a team, you create a robust support system that can contribute to your business's success. These advisors become your trusted allies, providing counsel on legal matters, financial strategies, and the nuances of entrepreneurship.

So, if you're passionate about your business venture, consider forming a Business Team of Mentors. Their collective wisdom can be a significant asset on your path to entrepreneurial success.

You as a Mentor

Finally, if you find joy in empowering others, I strongly encourage you to become a mentor.

In today's fast-paced world, many individuals have experienced a shift in family dynamics and support systems. The bonds that traditionally provided wise counsel and essential support may have weakened or even dissolved. In such a landscape, mentorship becomes a crucial avenue for offering guidance, wisdom, and support to those in need.

Mentoring allows you to share your knowledge, experiences, and insights with others who can benefit greatly from your guidance. It's an opportunity to provide a valuable connection and support system that may be missing from their lives.

By becoming a mentor, you not only contribute to the growth and development of others but also derive immense satisfaction from watching them flourish under your guidance. It's a rewarding endeavor that fosters personal and professional growth for both mentor and mentee.

So, if you have a desire to empower others and make a positive impact on their lives, consider stepping into the role of a mentor. Your guidance can be a beacon of light for someone.

How to Find a Mentor or Coach

Finding a mentor for your career can be a valuable step in your professional development. Here are some places and methods to help you find a mentor:

1. Workplace

Look within your current workplace for potential mentors. Senior colleagues or supervisors who have experience and expertise in your field can make excellent mentors. Don't be afraid to reach out and express your interest in learning from them.

2. Professional Associations

Many industries have professional associations or organizations. These groups often offer mentoring programs or events where you can connect with experienced professionals who are willing to mentor others in the field.

3. LinkedIn

Utilize LinkedIn to search for professionals in your industry or field who have the experience you admire. Send them a personalized message expressing your interest in learning from them. Be specific about what you hope to gain from the mentorship.

4. Networking Events

Attend industry-specific networking events, conferences, or seminars. These gatherings are excellent opportunities to meet potential mentors who share your professional interests. Engage in conversations and express your eagerness to learn from experienced individuals.

5. Online Mentorship Platforms

Some online platforms are dedicated to connecting mentors and mentees. Websites like LinkedIn, SCORE, or Mentoring.org can help you find mentors in various fields.

6. Alumni Associations

If you attended a college or university, your alma mater may have an alumni association that offers mentorship programs. Connect with fellow alumni who are willing to provide guidance.

7. Local Meetup Groups

Explore local meetup groups related to your industry or interests. These informal gatherings can introduce you to potential mentors who are passionate about helping others succeed.

8. Industry Conferences

Attend conferences specific to your field. These events often feature mentorship or networking sessions where you can connect with experienced professionals.

9. Professional Coaches

Consider hiring a professional coach or career counselor who specializes in mentorship. They can provide guidance tailored to your goals and aspirations.

10. Employee Resource Groups

If your workplace has employee resource groups (ERGs) or affinity groups, these can be excellent places to connect with mentors who share common backgrounds or interests.

11. Volunteer Organizations

Volunteering with organizations related to your career interests can introduce you to experienced professionals. They may be willing to mentor you based on shared values and causes.

12. Social Media and Forums

Engage in industry-related forums and social media groups. When approaching potential mentors, be respectful of their time and be open to their guidance and insights.

Chapter 7

Life Long Learning
&
Career Changing

""When you stop learning you start dying"
- Albert Einstein

Once upon a time, in a bustling city, lived a marketing executive named Sarah. She had been working in the same role for over a decade, and she was proud of her accomplishments. However, she noticed that the industry was rapidly changing due to the advent of digital marketing.

One day, Sarah attended a conference on digital marketing trends. As she sat among a sea of younger, tech-savvy professionals, she felt a bit out of her element. But instead of feeling discouraged, Sarah decided to embrace the opportunity to learn.

She started by attending workshops, webinars, and online courses on digital marketing during her free time. Sarah also subscribed to industry newsletters, read blogs, and followed influencers on social media. She even joined a professional association that focused on digital marketing.

Over the next few years, Sarah's knowledge and skills in digital marketing grew exponentially. She implemented new strategies and techniques in her job, and her campaigns started yielding better results. Her colleagues and superiors were impressed by her adaptability and willingness to learn.

Sarah's dedication to lifelong learning not only kept her job secure in the face of industry changes but also propelled her career to new heights. She eventually became the head of the digital marketing department and played a pivotal role in her company's success.

This anecdote illustrates that no matter where you are in your career, embracing lifelong learning can open doors to continuous growth and professional success.

Introduction

The wisdom encapsulated in this age-old adage. It underscores the importance of not only staying current within your area of expertise but also venturing beyond the boundaries of your comfort zone. Your journey of lifelong learning and personal growth can take many forms, each offering its unique rewards.

Expanding your knowledge can lead to potential career changes. This chapter delves into five avenues for pursuing lifelong learning and provides online resources where you can access valuable information for free. Additionally, it will conclude by examining various career change scenarios:

- Reading
- Webinars
- Educational Courses
- Think Beyond the Norm
- Career Transition

Resources to find Life Long Learning and Career Transitions are provided in the Appendices.

Reading

One of the most accessible and enriching ways to embark on your journey of personal development is through reading. Books have the power to inspire, educate, and expand your perspective. They offer a window into diverse worlds, providing insights and knowledge that can fuel your personal and professional growth.

Consider dedicating time to read books that resonate with you, whether they belong to your field of expertise or explore entirely different realms. The act of reading can stimulate your creativity, challenge your thinking, and open doors to new possibilities.

Webinars

Seminars and workshops are dynamic platforms that foster learning and networking. These events offer the opportunity to engage with experts in various fields, gain practical insights, and explore emerging trends. They provide a real-world context for applying knowledge and expanding your skill set.

Many associations and government bodies organize panel discussions, public forums, and seminars that are open to the public. Participating in these events not only broadens your understanding but also creates valuable business networking opportunities. By connecting with like-minded individuals and industry professionals, you enhance your support network and potential collaborations.

Educational Courses

Education is a lifelong pursuit, and enrolling in classes at various educational institutions can be a significant investment in your personal growth. Whether it's pursuing a formal degree, taking online courses, or attending workshops, education equips you with the tools and knowledge needed to thrive in an ever-evolving world.

These courses offer structured learning experiences that challenge you to think critically, solve complex problems, and adapt to changing circumstances. They empower you to acquire new skills, explore different fields, and discover hidden talents.

Incorporating these avenues of learning into your life not only keeps your mind engaged and curious but also cultivates a sense of vitality and purpose. Embrace the adage "To stop learning is to stop living" as a guiding principle on your journey toward continuous growth and fulfillment.

Think Beyond the Norm

Learning is the key that unlocks your mind, enabling you to venture beyond the confines of convention. It is within this realm of exploration that some of the most innovative Silicon Valley technology enterprises were born. Oftentimes, it begins with a simple thought: "If no one is hiring me, why not set up my own business and become the one who hires others?"

This thought process has yielded remarkable results, both in the realm of business and social impact. Consider my personal journey, early in my career. I aspired to sit on the Board of Directors of a not-for-profit organization, but when opportunities proved elusive, I decided to take matters into my own hands. I founded my own not-for-profit entity and formed a dedicated Board with myself as the Founder and Chair.

This shift in perspective is a testament to the power of learning and proactive thinking. It encourages us to challenge the status quo and explore alternative paths when traditional avenues seem closed. By embracing a mindset that values continuous learning and innovative thinking, we open doors to new possibilities, unearthing opportunities we may have never envisioned otherwise.

So, remember that learning is not merely an academic pursuit; it is a catalyst for personal and professional growth. It empowers you to think beyond the norm, paving the way for entrepreneurship, leadership, and the realization of your unique aspirations.

Career Changes and Transitions

Career changes refer to the significant shifts or transitions that individuals make in their professional lives, often involving a move from one field, industry, or job role to another. These changes can be motivated by various factors, such as personal growth, a desire for new challenges, changes in interests or values, economic conditions, or the pursuit of better opportunities.

Career changes can take several forms, including:

- **Change of Industry**

  Moving from one industry to another, such as transitioning from healthcare to technology or finance to education.

- **Change of Job Role**

  Shifting from one job role or function to another within the same industry or organization, like moving from a marketing role to a project management position.

- **Entrepreneurship**

  Starting a new business or venturing into self-employment after working in a traditional job.

- **Freelancing or Consulting**

  Transitioning from full-time employment to working as a freelancer or consultant in a specific field.

- **Retraining or Upskilling**

  Acquiring new skills or education to enter a different profession or industry.

- **Downshifting**

  Reducing work hours or responsibilities to achieve a better work-life balance.

- **Early Retirement**

  Retiring from a long-term career and then pursuing different interests or part-time work.

Career changes can be challenging, but they can also be incredibly rewarding when they align with an individual's passions, goals, and aspirations. Successful career changes often involve careful planning, self-assessment, acquiring relevant skills, networking, and sometimes seeking guidance from career counselors or mentors.

The Appendix J provides some scenarios to change the career.

Chapter 8

Harmonizing Life and Living

'*"The road to success and the road to failure are almost exactly the same." - Colin R. Davis

In a picturesque village nestled between rolling hills, there lived a man named Samuel. Samuel was a highly successful entrepreneur known for his thriving tech company. He had it all—wealth, a beautiful home, and a burgeoning career. However, his single-minded pursuit of business success had left little room for anything else in his life.

One summer evening, as Samuel sat alone on his lavish patio, he noticed his neighbor, Robert, tending to his lush garden. Robert was a retired schoolteacher who lived a simple and content life. Intrigued by the tranquility that seemed to surround Robert, Samuel struck up a conversation.

They spoke about their lives, and Robert shared his passion for gardening, painting, and volunteering at the local community center. Samuel, on the other hand, realized that his life had revolved solely around work, and he had neglected his own well-being and personal interests.

Inspired by his neighbor's wisdom, Samuel decided to make a change. He began dedicating more time to his family, taking long walks in nature, and exploring new hobbies. He even joined Robert at the community center as a volunteer.

Over time, Samuel's life transformed. While he continued to excel in his business, he found greater balance and fulfillment by embracing a more holistic approach. His relationships with family and friends deepened, and he discovered a newfound sense of purpose through his volunteer work.

As the years passed, Samuel became a role model for those around him, demonstrating that a well-rounded and holistic outlook on life not only enhances one's personal well-being but also leads to greater success and fulfillment in all aspects of life.

This story serves as a reminder that achieving success should encompass more than just professional accomplishments; it should include personal growth, relationships, and a balanced approach to living life to the fullest.

Introduction

While you invest your time and effort in advancing your career or nurturing your business pursuits, it's crucial to uphold a well-rounded (holistic) outlook on life.

The multifaceted nature of our existence encompasses seven key dimensions that profoundly impact our overall well-being. While your career and professional growth hold significance, they are but one piece of a larger puzzle:

1. **Finance**
   Your financial health plays a pivotal role in your quality of life. Managing your finances wisely, saving, investing, and planning for the future is integral components of your overall well-being.

2. **Relationships**
   Human connection forms the foundation of our emotional and social lives. Nurturing healthy relationships with family, friends, colleagues, and romantic partners enriches your existence.

3. **Personal Growth**
   Continual self-improvement and personal development are vital for intellectual and emotional growth. Seeking knowledge, refining your skills, and setting personal goals contribute to a fulfilling life.

4. **Career and Professional**
   Your career and professional pursuits hold a prominent place in your life. Achieving success in your chosen field, pursuing your passions, and honing your skills can bring immense satisfaction.

5. **Health & Wellness**
   Maintaining physical and mental well-being is paramount. Regular exercise, a balanced diet, proper sleep, and stress management are essential for a vibrant life.

6. **Home**
   Your living environment significantly influences your comfort and tranquility. A harmonious and organized home space contributes to a sense of stability and peace.

7. **Spirituality:** Exploring your spiritual beliefs and practices can provide a deeper sense of purpose and inner peace. It's a

dimension that nurtures your soul and fosters a connection to something greater than yourself.

As you navigate the intricacies of life, remember that these seven dimensions are interconnected, and they collectively shape your overall happiness and fulfillment. While career and professional growth are undoubtedly crucial, a well-rounded approach that addresses all aspects of your life ensures a more enriching and harmonious existence.

To achieve true success and happiness, it's imperative to strike a harmonious balance across all the dimensions of life mentioned above. You might be wondering how a holistic approach to life, emphasizing wellness, ties into the seven-step strategy for success. The connection is profound: success in your career alone cannot guarantee happiness if other aspects of your life remain neglected.

A robust spirit and a healthy heart form the cornerstone of a sound mind and body. Thus, it's essential to care for your physical well-being, adopting a holistic mindset that nurtures your mind, body, and soul. Neglecting your health, even in the face of professional success, can eventually erode your ability to pursue your dreams.

Remember that a state of wellness, both mentally and physically, brings equilibrium to your emotions and lifestyle.

Allow me to conclude with a story shared in the enduring best-seller, "The 7 Habits of Highly Effective People" (a book I wholeheartedly recommend to all). Stephen Covey recounts a tale of a man in a forest, laboriously sawing down a tree with a blunt saw. Despite his tireless efforts, he makes slow progress and grows increasingly frustrated. A passerby suggests that he take a break to sharpen his saw. The man, consumed by his task, retorts, "But I don't have time for that!"

Do you find yourself in a similar predicament? Covey's 7th Habit is refreshingly straightforward: take the time to rejuvenate, to sharpen your saw. How? Through exercise, meditation, journaling, quality time with loved ones, vacations, play, dance, indulging in your hobbies, and relishing life itself. Sharpen your tools for success, for as the old adage goes, "Work smarter, not harder."

Do the seven steps outlined in this book sound like hard work? Yes, they do require a recalibration of your approach. However, this journey can be made easier if you harbor a genuine passion for this seven-step strategy and wholeheartedly believe in it.

By applying this strategy, you may find that the journey itself can be as enjoyable as the destination, if not more so!

Finally, nothing is more important than your well-being. I appreciate the term "well-being" as it extends beyond mere physical health. I am not going to illustrate the significance of well-being compared to other aspects of life and living. I encourage you to take a moment to reflect and compare it to any aspect of your life. You might arrive at a similar realization!

"Nothing is more important than your well-being"

Appendices

A. Resources for Career and Entrepreneur Success

1. **LinkedIn Learning (formerly Lynda.com)**
   LinkedIn Learning offers a vast library of courses covering a wide range of topics, from leadership and business skills to technical skills and entrepreneurship.

2. **Coursera**
   Coursera partners with top universities and organizations to offer courses and specializations in business, entrepreneurship, leadership, and more. Many courses are free to audit, with the option to pay for a certificate.

3. **edX**
   Similar to Coursera, edX provides access to courses from universities and institutions worldwide. They offer courses in business, management, and entrepreneurship.

4. **Udemy**
   Udemy is an online learning platform that hosts thousands of courses on various topics, including business, entrepreneurship, marketing, and leadership.

5. **Small Business Administration (SBA)**
   The SBA's website provides a wealth of resources for entrepreneurs and small business owners, including guides, templates, and information on funding and loans.

6. **SCORE**
   SCORE is a non-profit organization that offers free mentoring and resources to small business owners and entrepreneurs. They have chapters across the United States.

7. **Entrepreneur.com**
   Entrepreneur.com is an online platform with articles, videos, and resources focused on entrepreneurship, start-ups, and small business management.

8. **Harvard Business Review**
   Harvard Business Review offers articles, podcasts, and videos on various business and leadership topics. They also have a paid subscription for more in-depth content.

9. **Fast Company**
   Fast Company is a business-focused magazine and website that covers innovation, leadership, and entrepreneurship. Their website offers articles and insights on these topics.

10. **TED Talks**
    TED Talks feature inspiring and informative talks from experts in various fields, including business and entrepreneurship. Many talks focus on leadership, creativity, and success.

11. **The Lean Start-up by Eric Ries**
    This book provides valuable insights into building and growing a start-up using lean principles. It's a must-read for aspiring entrepreneurs.

12. **The E-Myth Revisited by Michael E. Gerber**
    This book explores the common myths and misconceptions about starting a business and provides guidance on building a successful enterprise.

13. **Inc. Magazine**
    Inc. Magazine's website offers articles, tools, and resources for entrepreneurs and small business owners.

14. **Small Business Development Centers (SBDCs)**
    SBDCs provide free or low-cost consulting and training to help entrepreneurs and small business owners start and grow their businesses.

15. **Bplans**
    Bplans offers a wide range of business planning resources, including sample business plans, templates, and articles on business planning and strategy.

These resources can help you enhance your career, develop entrepreneurial skills, and succeed in your professional journey. Remember to tailor your learning and research to your specific career goals and needs.

B. Canadian Resources for Career and Entrepreneur Success

1. Government of Canada - Canada Business Network

- Website: Canada Business Network
- Description: Provides information and resources for starting, growing, and managing a business in Canada. Offers valuable guides and tools for entrepreneurs.

2. Business Development Bank of Canada (BDC)

- Website: BDC
- Description: BDC is a government-owned bank that provides financing, advisory services, and resources to Canadian entrepreneurs. They offer various guides and tools for business planning and growth.

3. Startup Canada

- Website: Startup Canada
- Description: A national network of entrepreneurs and organizations working to support and promote entrepreneurship in Canada. Offers resources, events, and networking opportunities.

4. Futurpreneur Canada

- Website: Futurpreneur Canada
- Description: Provides financing, mentorship, and resources to aspiring young entrepreneurs (aged 18-39) in Canada.

5. Canadian Federation of Independent Business (CFIB)

- Website: CFIB
- Description: Represents the interests of small and medium-sized businesses in Canada. Offers resources, research, and advocacy for business owners.

6. Women Entrepreneurs of Canada (WEConnect)

- Website: WEConnect Canada
- Description: Supports women-owned businesses by providing access to networks, resources, and opportunities for growth.

7. MaRS Discovery District

- Website: MaRS
- Description: MaRS is a Toronto-based innovation hub that offers resources, programs, and support for start-ups and entrepreneurs in various sectors.

8. Canadian Youth Business Foundation (CYBF)

- Website: CYBF
- Description: Provides mentorship, financing, and resources to young entrepreneurs in Canada.

9. Canadian Small Business Women

- Website: Canadian Small Business Women
- Description: Supports and empowers women entrepreneurs through networking events, workshops, and resources.

10. LinkedIn Canada

Website: LinkedIn Canada - Description: LinkedIn offers a platform for professional networking, job searches, and skill development. Joining relevant groups and following industry leaders can be beneficial for career growth.

11. Canadian Association of Management Consultants (CMC-Canada)

Website: CMC-Canada - Description: Provides resources and professional development opportunities for management consultants and those interested in management consulting careers.

12. Canada's Job Bank

Website: Canada's Job Bank - Description: A government job search tool that allows you to search for job opportunities across Canada, post your resume, and access labor market information.

13. Canadian Professional Sales Association (CPSA)
Website: CPSA - Description: Offers sales professionals access to resources, training, and certifications to enhance their sales careers.

14. Canadian Association of Marketing Professionals (CAMP)

Website: CAMP - Description: Supports marketing professionals by providing resources, networking events, and professional development opportunities.

These resources can help you navigate the Canadian business landscape, whether you're an entrepreneur looking to start or grow a business or a professional seeking career opportunities and development.

C. Books for Career and Entrepreneur Success

For Career Success

1. **"The 7 Habits of Highly Effective People" by Stephen R. Covey**
   o This classic offers principles for personal and professional effectiveness.
2. **"Mindset: The New Psychology of Success" by Carol S. Dweck**
   o Explores the importance of having a growth mindset for achieving success.
3. **"Lean In: Women, Work, and the Will to Lead" by Sheryl Sandberg**
   o Offers insights into women's careers and leadership in the workplace.
4. **"Drive: The Surprising Truth About What Motivates Us" by Daniel H. Pink**
   o Explores the science of motivation and how it relates to career success.
5. **"Grit: The Power of Passion and Perseverance" by Angela Duckworth**
   o Discusses the role of grit in achieving long-term goals and success.

For Entrepreneur Success:

1. **"The Lean Start-up: How Today's Entrepreneurs Use Continuous Innovation to Create Radically Successful Businesses" by Eric Ries**
   o Provides a methodology for building start-ups and launching products more efficiently.
2. **"Zero to One: Notes on Start-ups, or How to Build the Future" by Peter Thiel**
   o Offers unconventional thinking on start-ups and innovation.
3. **"Good to Great: Why Some Companies Make the Leap... and Others Don't" by Jim Collins**
   o Examines why certain companies excel and sustain long-term success.

4. **"The E-Myth Revisited: Why Most Small Businesses Don't Work and What to Do About It" by Michael E. Gerber**
    - Explores the myths and challenges of entrepreneurship and provides guidance for building a successful business.
5. **"Start with Why: How Great Leaders Inspire Everyone to Take Action" by Simon Sinek**
    - Focuses on the importance of defining the "why" behind your business to inspire others.

For Personal Development:

1. **"Atomic Habits: An Easy & Proven Way to Build Good Habits & Break Bad Ones" by James Clear**
    - Discusses how small changes in habits can lead to significant personal and professional growth.
2. **"Daring Greatly: How the Courage to Be Vulnerable Transforms the Way We Live, Love, Parent, and Lead" by Brené Brown**
    - Explores the power of vulnerability and courage in various aspects of life, including leadership.
3. **"Outliers: The Story of Success" by Malcolm Gladwell**
    - Analyzes the factors that contribute to high levels of success and achievement.
4. **"Emotional Intelligence: Why It Can Matter More Than IQ" by Daniel Goleman**
    - Explores the importance of emotional intelligence in personal and professional success.
5. **"The Power of Habit: Why We Do What We Do in Life and Business" by Charles Duhigg**
    - Examines the science of habit formation and how it impacts daily life and work.

These books cover a range of topics related to career, entrepreneurship, and personal development. Depending on your specific interests and goals, you can choose the ones that resonate with you the most to support your journey toward success.

D. Resources for Free Courses and Seminars

In today's digital age, the world of education and professional development has transcended physical boundaries, making knowledge and skills accessible to anyone with an internet connection. One remarkable facet of this accessibility is the wealth of free courses, seminars and workshops available online. These resources offer a plethora of learning opportunities that cater to diverse interests and professional growth objectives.

1. **Coursera (www.coursera.org)**
   Coursera is renowned for its comprehensive online courses from top universities and organizations. While some courses are paid, they also offer a selection of free courses on various subjects. These often include video lectures, assignments, and access to course materials.

2. **edX (www.edx.org)**
   Similar to Coursera, edX provides access to courses from universities worldwide. While many courses require payment for certification, auditing the course content is often free. It's an excellent platform for enhancing your knowledge and skills.

3. **MIT OpenCourseWare (ocw.mit.edu)**
   The Massachusetts Institute of Technology (MIT) offers a treasure trove of course materials from their actual classes. You can access lecture notes, assignments, and even video lectures for free. It's a fantastic resource for diving into technical subjects.

4. **Harvard Online Learning (online-learning.harvard.edu)**
   Harvard University provides free online courses across various disciplines. These courses often come with a certificate of completion that you can add to your professional portfolio.

5. **Khan Academy (www.khanacademy.org)**
   Khan Academy focuses on providing free educational content for learners of all ages. Their extensive library covers subjects ranging from math and science to humanities and economics.

6. **LinkedIn Learning** (www.linkedin.com/learning): LinkedIn Learning offers a vast library of video courses taught by industry experts. While it requires a subscription, you can access a one-month free trial to explore their content.

7. **Udemy** (www.udemy.com): Udemy hosts a diverse range of courses, and many instructors offer free courses as a way to introduce learners to their content. It's an excellent platform for exploring new topics.

8. **YouTube** (www.youtube.com): YouTube is a goldmine of educational content. Countless educators and organizations upload video tutorials, lectures, and workshops on a wide array of subjects. You can subscribe to channels that align with your interests.

9. **Eventbrite** (www.eventbrite.com): Eventbrite is a platform that lists a plethora of events, including free seminars and workshops. You can search for events based on your location and interests.

10. **Meetup** (www.meetup.com): Meetup is a platform that facilitates in-person and online gatherings for people with shared interests. Many groups organize free workshops and seminars that you can attend virtually.

These online resources for free seminars and workshops offer a diverse array of opportunities for personal and professional growth. Whether you're looking to enhance your skills, explore new subjects, or network with like-minded individuals, these platforms provide valuable avenues for self-improvement and learning.

E. Resources for Free e-books

1. **Project Gutenberg** (www.gutenberg.org): Project Gutenberg offers over 60,000 free e-books, including many classics. You can download these books in various formats, such as ePub, Kindle, and PDF.
2. **Google Books** (books.google.com): Google Books provides access to a vast collection of digitized books. While not all books are available for free, you can often preview significant portions or access older titles that have entered the public domain.
3. **Open Library** (openlibrary.org): Open Library offers access to millions of e-books, including rare and out-of-print titles. It's a fantastic resource for readers and researchers alike.
4. **Internet Archive** (archive.org): The Internet Archive hosts a vast digital library with millions of free books, as well as other media like movies, music, and more. It's a treasure trove for researchers and enthusiasts.
5. **BookBoon** (www.bookboon.com): BookBoon specializes in educational textbooks and business e-books. They offer a wide range of free, high-quality resources for students and professionals.
6. **ManyBooks** (manybooks.net): ManyBooks offers over 50,000 free e-books in various genres, including fiction, non-fiction, and self-help. You can download books in different formats.
7. **LibriVox** (librivox.org): LibriVox provides free audiobooks of classic literature. It's a volunteer-driven project, so you can enjoy listening to books while on the go.
8. **Smashwords** (www.smashwords.com): Smashwords is a platform that offers a vast collection of independently published e-books. Many authors provide their works for free or at discounted prices.
9. **BookFinder** (www.bookfinder.com): BookFinder is a search engine that helps you find new and used books, including rare and out-of-print editions. It's a useful tool for book enthusiasts.
10. **Amazon Kindle** (www.amazon.com): Amazon offers a selection of free e-books for Kindle users. You can explore their "Top 100 Free" section to discover free titles in various genres.

Remember to check the copyright status and terms of use for each resource, as availability may vary based on your location and the book's copyright status. Happy reading!

F. Resources for Groups and Forums

Participating in online groups and forums can be a great way to connect with like-minded individuals, share knowledge, and engage in discussions on various topics. Some of them have many millions users. Here are some online resources where you can find groups and forums to participate in:

1. **Reddit:** Reddit hosts numerous sub-reddits (topic-specific communities) on a wide range of subjects. You can find discussions on everything from technology to hobbies to professional advice. The website allows the member to post content e.g., links, texts, images, and even videos. These posts are then voted on by other members to rank them.

   Website: www.reddit.com

2. **Facebook Groups:** Facebook offers a plethora of groups covering various interests, hobbies, and professions. You can search for groups related to your specific area of interest.

   Website: www.facebook.com

3. **LinkedIn Groups:** LinkedIn has professional groups where you can engage in discussions related to your industry or area of expertise.

   Website: www.linkedin.com

4. **Stack Exchange:** Stack Exchange is a network of Q&A communities where you can ask and answer questions on a wide range of topics, including technology, science, and more.

   Website: stackexchange.com

5. **Quora:** Quora is a platform for asking questions and sharing knowledge on various subjects. You can follow topics and engage in discussions with experts.

   Website: www.quora.com

6. **Meetup:** Meetup helps you find and build local communities. You can search for groups and events in your area related to your interests.

    Website: www.meetup.com

7. **Discord:** Discord is a communication platform primarily used by gamers, but it has expanded to cover various interests. You can find servers (communities) related to specific topics.

    Website: discord.com

8. **GitHub Discussions:** If you're interested in coding and development, GitHub Discussions offers forums for open-source projects and programming languages.

    Website: github.com/discussions

9. **Hacker News:** Hacker News is a forum for tech enthusiasts, entrepreneurs, and developers to discuss the latest technology and start up news.

    Website: news.ycombinator.com

10. **Goodreads Groups:** If you're a book lover, Goodreads has various groups where you can discuss books and literary topics.

    Website: www.goodreads.com

A recommendation of 17 Online Community Platforms: https://www.thinkific.com/blog/best-online-community-platforms/

When participating in online groups and forums, remember to follow the community guidelines and engage respectfully. These platforms can be valuable resources for learning, networking, and sharing your knowledge and expertise.

G. Miscellaneous Resources

Registration of domain names:
https://blog.hubspot.com/website/how-to-register-domain-name

Discover a personalized website package inclusive of your own email address, offered by a friendly company. Don't forget to mention the book's name to secure a generous discount.
https://www.iqwebsolutions.com/

H. Top Ten Career Change Ideas by Duke Duyck

Career changes can be challenging, but they can also be incredibly rewarding when they align with an individual's passions, goals, and aspirations. Successful career changes often involve careful planning, self-assessment, acquiring relevant skills, networking, and sometimes seeking guidance from career counselors or mentors.

1. **MEDITATION**
   - Have faith in your destiny, your karma, your personal life goal.
   - You may get what you need, if not what you want.
   - Imagine the job that is best for your unique self, without forcing your preconceived ideas/education to direct you.

2. **ASSESS**
   - Your education, training, skills, experience, expertise in view of future markets, obsolescence and new environment
   - Your re-certification requirements
   - Budget and financial planning
   - Location relative to the job opportunities and future market

3. **FORWARD VIEW**
   - Opportunities in new markets
   - Growing businesses with their eyes on the future
   - Businesses that will need your specific unique skills

4. **FLEXIBILITY**
   - Avoid preconceived ideas about your job, profession, type of work
   - Expect to change from the past
   - Imagine the future of your skills and prepare for changing in that direction
   - Be prepared to learn what will be needed later
   - Be prepared to switch your profession or industry by learning a new one
   - Be prepared to be a change agent
   - Be ready to provide a service that will be in demand tomorrow

5. **SELLING YOURSELF**
   - Taylor your resume/portfolio to the target NOT general
   - What you can do for the company
   - Accomplishments in terms of their needs
   - Education and skills in terms of what they need

6. **USE DIFFERENT METHODS TO FIND A JOB**
   -Ads
   -Networking
   -Cold calling (Don't ask for a job, but for 'advice' for
      opportunities anywhere)
   -Apply inside the workplace for higher job
   -Market research for new kind of jobs with high demand/ low
      supply expertise + acquire that expertise
   -Apply for temp job for sideways move in future - foot in the
      door technique
   -Use a temp job to get money for bread and training
   -Try multiple sources of income, but leave enough time for
      re-training
   -Work as a contractor, your own business (consider tax
      implications)

7. **DO RESEARCH ON THE PROSPECTS**
   -Know who is who
   -Know their financial status
   -Know their needs
   -Expect questions and prepare answers
      o Lack of experience - know how to bring in new
         ideas and education
      o Re-certification - when
      o Re-location - willingness
      o Salary, fringes n perks
      o Management experience
      o Why did you leave
      o Why did you apply here
      o Your objectives – where do you see yourself in x
         years

8. **PLAN FOR WHO YOU TALK TO**
   -Recruiter
   -HR
   -Manager
   -President
   -Owner

9. AVOID
- Lock into any low paying job that does not allow for training and job search time
- Jobs where you cannot be unique – like being one of many
- Pyramid schemes (MLS)
- Negative influences, friends and environments that give you bad reputation.
- Excessive commuting
- Unaffordable loans
- Burning you bridges
    - The company you left may make you a better offer
  - The company that rejected you may come back with an offer later

10. PLANNING ACCEPTANCE/REJECTION
- Take your time to view all angles
- Don't sell yourself too cheap
- Have a point system for trade-offs
- Temp conditions vs future
- Opportunities for change
- Time table of changes
- What will the job be in 5 years
- Chances of promotion
- Outside market
- Competition
- Working environment
- Enjoyment of the work
- Being motivated
- Opportunities for learning
- A job vs a career
- Your home and family life
- Travel and commuting
- Responsibility and authority
- Freedom and trust
- Present salary vs future
- Salary vs fringes and perks
- Salary vs commission

Duke Duyck, P.Eng. Retired from being a Profitability Analyst and Consultant.
He is a Toastmaster and presently occupied in various volunteer positions, dealing with leadership, career, financial management and income taxes. He is also in the process of writing about his profitability expertise and experiences

I. About the Healthy Aging Foundation (HAF)

The Healthy Aging Foundation (HAF) is a federally registered non-profit organization dedicated to promoting education on healthy aging and the science of longevity. Our mission is to disseminate well-researched and often inaccessible knowledge to the public through educational initiatives, symposiums, and publications.

We recognize the abundance of research and scientific advancements in the field of healthy aging. Our goal at HAF is to bridge the gap between this knowledge and individuals at the local and personal levels through engaging discussions and informative publications. While we do not conduct research ourselves, we serve as a platform for delivering valuable insights.

At HAF, our motto is to 'Empower You by Sharing Knowledge and Wisdom.'

Demographics
Seniors represent the fastest-growing age group in North America and worldwide. By the year 2026, seniors are projected to make up over one-fifth of the population. As research consistently predicts an increase in longevity, it becomes increasingly important to prioritize living healthier lives throughout our lifespan.

The Healthy Aging Institute (HAI) and LIFE-TALKS are educational initiatives launched by the Healthy Aging Foundation (HAF).

Our Projects
In light of the challenges posed by the pandemic, we have identified gaps in our understanding of maintaining good health. To address this, we have undertaken the following initiatives:

1. **Books**: We cover various health topics in our publications, providing accessible information for readers.
2. **Life-Talks:** We invite researchers and health practitioners from diverse treatment modalities, including conventional medicine, to share their insights through engaging speaker sessions.
3. **Rejuvenate Retreats**: Join us for a week-long Detox Retreat in a blue-zone environment, where you can revitalize your mind and body.
4. **Healthy Aging Basic Workshops:** These workshops feature professional PowerPoint presentations and handouts, providing essential information on healthy aging.

If you are a health practitioner in any modality or an author, we encourage you to contribute and participate in the above projects.

Become a Part of Our Legacy
 We invite you to become a part of our organization and support our mission. There are several ways you can get involved:

1. Become an Associate Member.
2. Become a Professional Member.
3. Become a Corporate Member.
4. Become a Sponsor and Partner with us in our endeavours.

Let us evolve together.
Max Haroon, Founder and President
info@healthyaging.foundation, 416-891-4937, healthyaging.foundation

J: About the Author, Max Haroon

Max Haroon is a multifaceted individual with a diverse range of passions and experiences. He is a social entrepreneur, author, and speaker who is deeply passionate about holistic health and integrative medicine. As the founder of the Healthy Age Foundation (HAF), Max Haroon has been instrumental in advocating for a holistic approach to health and well-being.

In addition to his work in the field of health and wellness, Max Haroon has enjoyed a distinguished career spanning over 35 years in the Information Technology (IT) industry, with experience in Europe, the Middle East, and Asia.

He has worked in various sectors, including the Internet and IT Training, and has been a prominent figure in promoting the effective use of the Internet for personal and professional growth.

Max Haroon is renowned for his engaging and informative speaking engagements at conferences and symposiums. Over the years, he has hosted numerous social, technical and educational events, including workshops and conferences, dating back to 1985.

Max Haroon has played a founder role in the establishment of several community organizations, associations, and non-profit initiatives, such as:

1. Society of Internet Professionals (SIP)
2. Neighbourhood Watch
3. Inspirational Book Club
4. Holistic Food Institute
5. Life Transformation Institute

His commitment to sharing knowledge and fostering personal development is evident in his extensive public speaking and event-hosting endeavors.
As an accomplished author, Max Haroon has authored many publications, both in print and online, covering a wide range of topics.

His Webfolio, available at www.maxharoon.org, provides further insights into his work and areas of expertise. For inquiries and further communication, you can reach him at contact@maxharoon.org.

K. Publications by Max Haroon

7 Steps to Dental Health
A Holistic Guide for a Healthy Mouth & Body
While you may encounter adults living without chronic diseases and enjoying full mobility, it's a rare sight to find them with a complete set of original, healthy teeth. This book delves into the reasons behind this and explores how to attain excellent oral health, which in turn contributes to overall well-being.

Planning for the Final Chapter
End-of-Life Caring and Peaceful Passing
How many of us actually plan for the last stage of our lives?
This guide aims to underscore the importance of making deliberate decisions for this final passage while we still possess the capacity to do so.
The book organizes all processes into three main categories: Estate Planning, Health and Caring Planning, and Dealing with Events after Death.

Charting Your Path to Professional Success
A Seven-Step Guide for Job Seekers and Entrepreneurs
This book is a culmination of years of experience delivering talks at various job conferences and job fairs. It is primarily geared toward newcomers and recent graduates, individuals who are not only embarking on their careers but often doing so in a new country. The initial edition of this book was written between 2007 and 2012, and its timeless wisdom serves as a steadfast blueprint for career building. The revised 2023 edition incorporates a wealth of online resources integrated into each chapter.

Seven Steps to Reboot Your Well-Being
Understanding the Causes of Sickness and Pillars of Well-Being
This book will provide a framework by various practitioners, based on the principle that our body has inherent power to heal us without/minimal external interventions. We are assembling seven practitioners from different modalities, like Homeopathy, Allopathic (Medicine and Dental), Traditional Chinese Medicine, Ayurvedic, Herbalist, Clinical Nutritionist, Energy Healers and more. Each contributor will provide their insight and protocols according to their experience and background.

Nurturing Living Food

7 Ways to Cultivate Your Own Enzymes and Vitamins
Eating raw or living food is an excellent healthy eating habit. There are a few delicious ways to eat raw living plant based foods like Sprouting, Soaking, Growing Green or Grass, Fermentation

The Black book of Event Planning and Management

Methodology of Event Planning and Management in Seven Steps
Master, the Life Cycle of an event by breaking it into phases, tasks, documents and bind it with a committed Event team and apps. This guide is based on my 20 years experince and methodology used to run run events for the Society of Internet Professionals (SIP).

L. Acknowledgments

The original editor of this writing in 2012 was Di Wright, a Business Communications Specialist, Career Coach, and Writer. Unexpectedly, Duke Duyck stepped in for meticulous editing of my revised work, for which I am sincerely thankful.

I'd like to extend my special thanks to my reviewers, especially Kashif Iqbal and Duke Duyck.

Contrary to popular belief, people do judge a book by its cover. Therefore, I am deeply appreciative of Kashif Iqbal for designing the book's cover..